Flawed Landscape

W9-BMO-167

Flawed Landscape

POEMS 1987–2008

SHARIF S. ELMUSA

Interlink Books

An imprint of Interlink Publishing Group, Inc.
Northampton, Massachusetts

First published in 2008 by

INTERLINK BOOKS
An imprint of Interlink Publishing Group, Inc.
46 Crosby Street, Northampton, Massachusetts 01060
www.interlinkbooks.com

Text copyright © Sharif S. Elmusa 2008

All rights reserved. No part of this publication may be reproduced, stored in a retrieval system, or transmitted in any form or by any means, electronic, mechanical, photocopying, recording, or otherwise without the prior permission of the publisher.

Library of Congress Cataloging-in-Publication Data
Elmusa, Sharif, 1947-
Flawed landscape: poems 1987-2008 / by Sharif S. Elmusa. -- 1st American ed.
  p. cm.
ISBN 978-1-56656734-3 (pbk.)
I. Title.
PR93759.E46F53 2008
811'.6--dc22
                    2008022754

Cover image by George Azar

The author thanks the editors of the following publications in which many of the poems in this collection have previously appeared, not always with identical titles or texts.

Alif: Journal of Contemporary Poetics 20 (2000): "Moons and Donkeys: Fragments from the Gaza Strip"; *Alif* 27 (2007) "The Little Prince and the Air Force Pilot"; *Anthology of Modern Palestinian Literature*, edited by Salma Khadra Jayyusi (New York: Columbia University Press, 1992) "A Little Piece of Sky," "In Balance"; *Banipal* (Autumn/Winter 2002/3) "What Makes the Man?," "Life Was Roughly Right," "With New Englanders," "To Feel Their Humiliation"; *Cedar Rock* (Spring 1984) "The Two Angels," "Expatriates"; *Christian Science Monitor* (2 April 1986) "She Fans the Word"; *Grape Leaves: A Century of Arab-American Poetry*, edited by Gregory Orfalea and Sharif S. Elmusa (Northampton: Interlink Books, 2000) "The Two Angels," "Snapshots," "In the Refugee Camp," "Expatriates," "Dream on the Same Mattress"; *Greenfield Review* 13.1 & 2 (1985) "Snapshots"; *I Feel a Little Jumpy Around You*, edited by Naomi Shihab Nye and Paul B. Janeczko (New York: Simon and Schuster, 1996): "A Little Piece of Sky"; *New Letters* 60.3 (1995) "Epitaph for a Mass Grave in Sabra and Shatila"; *Poetry East* 29 (Winter 1988) "In the Refugee Camp"; *Poetry Ireland Review* 75 (Winter 2002/3) "Homeward Bound"; *Post-Gibran: Anthology of New Arab-American Writing*, edited by Khaled Mattawa and Munir Akash (Syracuse, NY: Syracuse University Press, 1999) "Flawed Landscape," "Soliloquy"; *Ruah* X (2000) "The Two Angels," "But I Heard the Drops," "Flawed Landscape," "Haven't You Found My Brother in America?" "How Things Migrate," "Like Early Man," "Yearning"; *The Space Between Our Footsteps*, edited by Naomi Shihab Nye (New York: Simon and Schuster, 1998) "Snapshots," "But I Heard the Drops," "A Day in the Life of Nablus."

In memory of my friends

Bushra Qaraman

Lamis Jarrar

Sami Suleiman

Who died before their time

─────────────────────────────── PART THREE

Flawed Landscape

PART ONE

War takes us lightly.
—Georges Bataille

What Makes the Man?

What makes the man
who meanders,
like an uncertain river,
before deciding
what to have for dinner
which film to see
when he last had a haircut—
what makes this man
close one eye
aim intently
through the scope of his rifle
and become the most precise,
the most direct of animals?

The Little Prince and the Air Force Pilot

"You should have seen the imploded children
you have killed in your last air raid,"
said the little prince to the air force pilot
he had chanced on planet F52.

> "I did not mean to kill children,
> when I dropped the bombs,"
> answered the pilot.

"If you had not meant to kill them,
why, then, did you let your bombs fall
on a tall building, full of apartments?
Apartments are where children live
like bees live in beehives
and birds live in nests on the trees,
and ants in anthills.
What a lethal life you lead."

> Unfazed, the pilot retorted,
> "I was after the monsters
> who hid in the building."

"May I point out,"
said the little prince,
pointing his forefinger at the pilot,
"children are children,
they spend their time bonding
with important toys and ball games;

they cannot be responsible
for who lives with them in the building."

Still, deeply upset, the little prince turned
to the small fox lying by his feet;
and, without preface, he said,
"the logic of grown-ups is odd, isn't it?"

Flawed Landscape

And it came to pass,
we lost the war, and became a nation of refugees.
It is always the beginning.
Fueled by fear, my father gathered
the clan, lugged me in his arms,
and headed, on his peasant feet,
across plain and impassable mountain,
without a compass, headed east.

We set down in a camp in a desert,
without the sinuous sands of the movies,
by the gateless town of Jericho.
In that flawed landscape,
under the shadow of the dark rocks
of the Mount of Temptation,
the world was kind to us.
The United Nations, our godfather,
doled out flour and rice and cheddar,
"yellow," cheese—sharp beyond our palettes.

My father remembered his twelve olive trees
every day for ten years. He remembered
the peasants saying to the olive tree,
Had she felt for their toil,
she'd yield not olives, but tears,
and the tree answering,
Tears you have enough; I give you oil
to light your lamps, to nourish, and to heal.

Then one day he let go. Let go.
My father was no Ulysses.
He found a new land, and stayed away
on the farm, eking out some rough happiness.

My mother stayed home.
Shepherded a pack of twelve, cleaned and yelled
and, for punishment, summoned father's shadow.
She stuffed our thin bones with sentiments,
as if to makes us immobile.

Her past was insatiable:
The new house they had just built,
windows on four sides, tall and arched,
to let in the ample light,
to spread out the prayers;
how my father rushed to ask for her hand
the day after she had kept him in line
at the water well; how they found
the body of her brother soaked
in sweet-scented blood,
at the police station,
after he had been killed by the discriminate bullets
of the British soldiers.

No statues were built in the camp;
the dead would have been ashamed.
The living dreamed—the dreams of the wounded.
In their houses the radio was the hearth,
                          and news the oracle.

In the Refugee Camp

The huts were made of mud and hay,
their thin roofs feared the rain,
and walls slouched like humbled men.
The streets were laid out in a grid,
as in New York,
but without the dignity of names
or asphalt. Dust reigned.
Women grew pale
chickens and children
feeding them fables from the lost land.
And a madman sawed the minaret
where a melodious voice
cried for help on behalf of the believers.

Of course I gazed at the sky
on clear nights,
at stars drizzling
soft grains of light,
at the moon's deliberate face,
at the good angel wrapped in purple air.
                    I had no ladder
and nothing from heaven fell
in my crescent hands.

Ah, how I cursed Adam and Eve
and the One who made them refugees.

An Epitaph for a Mass Grave in Sabra and Shatila

Our defenders left us
after we had been promised safety.
But we were gunned down,
bludgeoned by axes, hoes,
by nocturnal cowardice.

Mothers and fathers
brothers and sisters
friends and neighbors—
the bulldozers hurled us all
into this fast-dug hole,
hurled us all at once
the earth was so dumbfounded—
it could not cry: "Enough."

We lie now, like all the dead,
in vast repose.

When you come by
please say a prayer
then keep quiet,
keep quiet.

To Feel the Humiliation

Today I have seen of war
all I want to see.

A row of men with blindfolded eyes
and surrendered hands
squat, backs hunched,
before a stone wall.

A young boy stays home
for five days, alone,
with the corpses of his family.

A man gestures, with loathing,
about how a soldier had defecated
on his bed. An old woman flails
her arms in despair, begging
the distant heavens.

To feel the humiliation,
to touch the grief of each
I would have to become a monster
with many hearts.

Life was Roughly Right

The last time I saw my cousin, Miqdad,
before this last war, he was back home
for good from the rich Gulf. There, he circulated,
imperfectly, tending the business of men
with superior luck. To make the worth
of his long migration visible, he built a house,
a handsome house on a hilltop,
the essential dish raised over the red-tiled roof,
netting the news—the chewing *qat* of Palestine.

He said life was roughly right.
He cherished the drizzle of each day:
dinner served on time, a kid's good grade,
the marigolds' longevity in the austere garden.

With his sharp face and something always in his hand,
he looked like a figure in an Ancient Egyptian relief
presenting, with singular delight, an offering to the god.

But the soldiers weren't invited.
They banged on the metal door of the house
and kicked it with their boots
and when he opened it they made him turn
and stuck the gun into his back.
They used him as "a human shield,"
to search the house, room after neat room,
and made him dig with a hoe
they had fetched from an armored car

the earth-fill of what used to be a cistern
where he might have hidden arms.

The next day a blood clot clogged
the left side of his brain.
His eyelids are now lowered, at half-mast;
the few words he utters
are hieroglyphic fish and birds.

The Eraser

In the beginning, the Eraser razed the village.

He let the villagers be frightened into fleeing,
their houses and their fields,
and He saw that they had fled,

and He heard the ghosts talking
strange talk in the empty houses,

and He let the houses be rubble, without form,
and let the stray animals roam the site,
and He saw that the sight was an unnecessary reminder,

and He let there be a forest of native trees
rise above and cover the debris,
and He saw that the forest was like a natural growth,

and He let a sign rise on the side
of the highway, bearing the site's new name,
and He saw that the new name derived from his own tale,

and He let the old name be expunged
from His kingdom's maps and encyclopedias
and He saw that the old name was gone,

and He saw all that He unmade and, O wow,
was it good and, on the sixth day, He took a break.

Waking up on the seventh day,
He saw that the refugees had multiplied
and become fabulists, conjuring forest fires.

With New Englanders

I miss my Boston dentist.
The first time I met him,
before injecting the Novocain
into my anxious gums,
he paused
and asked where I was from.
From Palestine, I answered.
"How is the weather in Palestine?"
he wanted to know.

The weather there is temperate,
soil terra rosa.
The shepherds on the hills
have all but disappeared.
Winter sends modest rains,
animates the hardened earth:
red poppies swaying in the breeze,
little spokesmen of beauty;
cotton flowers, purple,
the sting of their thorns
final, like the rebellious gestures of Jesus.

Summer's sun is perpendicular.
The old man would be dejected
without cartloads of watermelons.
No blunt pleasures.
Season blends into season
in good faith.

With New Englanders
you muffle the sandstorms.

A Day in the Life of Nablus

We fall, not on our knees, but on our hearts

—Vassar Miller

Summer. The figs are bruise pink,
tomatoes luscious enough
to stop a hurried man.
Ignore the flies.
At 9 a.m. peasants savor shish-kebab
in puny, vaulted eateries.
Ah, the roasting coffee's aroma,
the folklore of each of the senses.

Everything here is for sale:
children's toys, kitchen utensils,
bananas, peanuts, pine nuts, posters,
cassettes, straw mats, sponge mats, watches,
Elvis's T-shirts, turkey breasts, shoes.

The vendor in disheveled clothes
arranges a feast of pears,
lifts one with pride
as he might his own child.
He bellows into the air:
"Go to sleep with a sweet mouth."
He sees the soldiers.
He does not brood over power or history.

No curfew
during our five-week stay.

❧

Walking on University Boulevard,
I spot soldiers manning a checkpoint:
the school has been ordered shut.
And, as if in the recurring dream,
I frisk myself for my passport
but find my pockets empty.
I go past the black machine guns
thinking how as a boy
I caught black wasps
and removed their stingers.

A few yards away from the checkpoint
I read a sign:
Office of Reconciliation.
Inside, a Samaritan rabbi
clad in brown caftan and red turban
is ensconced on a couch, waiting,
resigned to waiting.

❧

On an immaculate wall
of a friend's living room
hangs a picture in a gilded frame:
a woman squatting amidst the rubble
of her house demolished by the army,

cheek cupped in hand,
peering into a white, empty bucket.

❧

In cafés men congregate in the afternoons,
slowly sip their tea
(as if time were their own),
shuffle cards, spur the backgammon dice
(as if chance were their own).
They listen to songs
of unrequited love, broken promises, partings.
When the sun sinks behind the hills
they salute the fading day, irreconciled,
leaving the folded market
to the screech of armored cars.

❧

The sky flowers tonight.
The stars are as bright and real
as children's eyes
as the faces of women loved
after years of waiting.
A meteor dives like a deft acrobat.
A satellite sails west to east, unperturbed.
Russian or American?
Scientist or spy? Or

a station where voices
of distant lovers dovetail?

In gowns of soft lights
the town performs the ritual of sleep.
Will they caress the mouth of the vendor,
and the silence of the woman who lost her house?
The settlement, fortress on the mountain peak,
and the jail on the hilltop
flood their sleep with yellow lights.

I want the kind breeze
the power of pears
the sound of the flute,
melodious and sad,
like the hills of this land,
to grant us all,
vendors and soldiers,
grant us ample love
that we may turn this troubled page
that we may sleep with a sweet mouth.

Moons and Donkeys

Gaza is a cage,
barb-wired on the inland sides;
the sea mostly off limits.
No mountains, no valleys,
the place is flat.
Forget about movies, books and bars.
The war is said to be over, the price paid,
and will be paid further.
A torpid peace is settling in.
What were the Prophets smitten by?

I am told
The yellow finches
perch on the fence,
consider,
smell the rampant sewers
then wing back to the desert.

I go around,
like an ancient Chinese poet,
watching moons and donkeys.

❧

A man who lived for many years in Norway,
told me that on the first day back here
he went out for a walk
when, a few blocks from his parents' house,

two old men and two middle-aged women
sitting in a row on low chairs on the curb,
caught in boredom's web,
unleashed their eight eyes on him,
with such penetrating, persistent stares
he began to scan his shirt and pants,
and feel his face with his agitated hand
to find out what was wrong with him,

until he almost stumbled.

❧

"The longest part of the journey is said to be the passing of
the gate," thus Marcus Teertius Varro.

This is Eretz checkpoint, the northern gate of Gaza, a fortress
of concrete blocks, barbed wire, and soldiers: young men in
seaweed-green fatigues, as clean and charged as their guns.

The man crossing the gate was dead, a student who had died in
Moscow and was brought home for burial. His coffin was
hauled from the airport in an ambulance, attended by a cousin.
At the proper booth, the driver handed a soldier the requisite
documents for passage. The soldier told the driver and the
cousin that the coffin too must be X-rayed.

The cousin reluctantly yielded to the order. He and the
driver slid the coffin onto the machine, but only a part of the
coffin could fit in at once: the machine was short, the coffin
long. The first part done, the driver turned the ambulance

around to face the other side of the machine. When the two men tried to insert the second half of the coffin through the door of the machine, they discovered the door was too narrow. And the coffin was hung between the ambulance and the machine.

A moment or, as it must have seemed to the cousin, an eternity in limbo. For soon, as though drawing the line of his tolerance, he yelled at the soldiers, in Hebrew, to leave the dead man in peace. A row ensued. Then the soldiers manipulated the door of the machine, and the coffin was all X-rayed, cleared. The cousin was detained, for questioning. The ambulance sped away with the body, the dust in its wake tossing away the shreds of a newspaper.

&

Again, Eretz checkpoint, and another rite of passage. I was going with a friend to Jerusalem in her white UN jeep. On the way out, the jeep, like all vehicles leaving Gaza, had to be inspected. A soldier asked my friend to open the hood. She was new here and hadn't opened the hood before. She looked for the handle under the instrument panel, and couldn't find it. Then I tried, to no avail.

A soldier came in and couldn't locate it either. He called another uniformed man who told us he was a mechanic. The mechanic also searched, in vain. My frustrated friend said maybe Madeline Albright could help (she was in Jerusalem that day). We all laughed. I had been through Israeli check-points countless times before, without the soldiers ever lowering their guard and allowing a casual exchange that might make the guns momentarily invisible. But this time—thanks to the mysterious Japanese design, my friend's inexperience and the common purpose of wanting to open the hood—a modicum of humanity intruded between us. Not enough to let us through, though.

When it began to seem like an impasse, my friend pulled her cell phone out of her purse and called a coworker. The mechanic asked if he could speak to him; of course, she said (what choice did she have, really?). He said the coworker told him the handle was inside the glove compartment; and straight he went and opened the glove compartment; and there it was, the handle.

❧

After a few weeks
the spirit corrugated,
like the rooftops in the refugee camps.
My feet walked backward,
like the feet of the shoeless children.

❧

At dawn
the muezzins' megaphones
clash, overlap,
each spurred on—
to call us, louder,
and louder—for prayer,

to amplify to God
our impotence.

❧

The ash-colored donkey
was pregnant and flaunting it—
belly full, hanging low
like the night's moon.
She stepped into the road,

slowly, deliberately,
then balked. Turned
her head this way and that.
All the honking fell on deaf ears.
I watched from my stopped car
this mock checkpoint
this street theater.

❧

I want to cross borders
unseen
like salmon
like contaminated wind.

❧

Once Jeha lived by the borderline between two countries,
which suited him well because he worked as a smuggler.
Everyday he crossed the border in the morning and

returned in the evening, leading a donkey freighted with goods. The customs officials inspected the load, found nothing contraband and let him go. Jeha made the daily excursion for thirty years, then retired to the city, a rich man.

Upon his retirement, he began to build a luxurious house, commensurate with his wealth. While he was at the site one day, a customs officer recognized him. The officer approached him and greeted him and inquired whether he had changed his job and become a construction worker. Jeha answered, No, he was retired and supervising the workers building his own house. The officer couldn't believe it, and told Jeha he must be kidding, a poor man with a donkey couldn't afford such a fabulous mansion. Jeha retorted, he in fact was rich, from all the smuggling. The officer said, "Come on, you couldn't have been a smuggler, we inspected your donkey's load every time. What did you smuggle, man?" Jeha replied, "Well, I smuggled donkeys."

🫏

The corpse of a huge beast
lay in the middle of a boulevard.
Crushed watermelons were strewn
all around. Bands of women
waving banners
with the word METAPHYSICAL
marched down the curbs;
they had no legs, only shoes.

On the rooftops first appeared snipers;
soon the barrels of their rifles

morphed into bamboo flutes.
From the side streets
a carnival of men and women,
barely dressed,

flowed into the boulevard,
gyrating from hip to toe
to invisible drums.
I followed them, braying with lust,
like a he-donkey.

One woman winked at me,
"See you in the spring,"
and kept dancing. The sun was vertical,
and I soaked in sweat. Someone blurted out:
"All of this and it's hardly noon."

❧

Scores of fishing boats
          spread out
                    of the meager port.
In the depth of the night
          their kerosene lamps
                    an oasis of lights,
soft, yellow—
          a beauty
                    hard to conquer
or resist.

The fishermen doze off,
          then row again.

❧

A crescent moon gleamed,
rocked, like a gondola.
The orthodox clouds
marched on, and covered it.

❧

A daily summer ritual.
A wedding motorcade
in the late afternoon:
A few cars (for the lucky ones),
a bus, and a pickup truck or two
packed with young boys
who laugh and dance,
clap and sing,
like birds singing
to make themselves visible
in the cage.

PART TWO

My mother counts my twenty fingers from afar.
—Mahmoud Darwish

Birth

I cried my first small cry
on April 12, 1947, mother's estimate,
two weeks before my cousin
whose birth certificate survived the war.
Because the cry was a boy's
it was amplified by ululations, mounds
of buttered rice and Turkish delight.

The village, Abbasiyya (not Abbysinia),
lay far enough from the sea
not to spawn sailors,
close enough to have horizon.
The highway made a small gesture
to its modest homes.

My parents tilled the red earth,
their young backs stooped over it,
made it articulate with oranges and grapes.
They fenced the fields with cactus plants
and *ma-wa-weel*, blues,
hearty as molasses, cutting
as the hoe's edge.

They groped one night
toward each other, tired,
a starlight stealing through the cracks
in the door. They wished for a son
to secure their old age,
to leaven their pleasure.

Dream on the Same Mattress

Welcome
to the tribe of the wed.
But before you enter
                the tent
let me stitch a patch or two
                onto your quilt.

Resilience,
a shrewd caliph once said,
is the golden rule
                of politics.
Resilience, my kinsfolk,
is the diamond rule
                of marriage.
This cord of love
that binds you now
    keep it taut—
give when she pulls
    and pull when he gives.
Marriage is a rose garden
where squash is fond to grow.
        Accept them both:
The spirit seeks
                inspiration
and the stomach
                sustenance.

Do not eat from the same dish,
said Gibran,

                but the prophet never married.
Drink from the same cup,

                                    I say,
and dream on the same mattress.

She Fans the Word

(*For Karmah*)

A word
            round and full
finally blooms
            on the raw tongue
                    of the child.
It makes her giddy.
She fans the word
by her bear
            and bunny
by the flowers
            in the vase
by the strange forms
            in the mirror
by the water
            breaking loose
                    from the hose.
She fans the word
            as a peacock fans
                    its tail
as a man his windfall,
            unsure of having,
                    afraid of losing it.

Like Early Man

Reading Layth a story,
I watch its magic dissolve
in the white of his smile
in the blue of his faraway eyes.
One day he will figure out the moral.

I tuck him in bed
next to the soft blue light
of the globe. I observe the names
of cities and countries,
borders in red lines,
longitudes and latitudes,
the mental hoops that make us believe
the Earth belongs to us.

In which language will death
order me to acquiesce?
Where will the ghosts
in the neighboring graves come from?
Will the necromancer be able
to pronounce my name?
It doesn't matter in the grave.

I watch our picture on the wall,
my hand bracing him,
to keep him from falling off
the branch of the blossoming cherry tree.
Or is it he bracing me?

I fall asleep by his side
with one eye open,
like early Man.

One Pillow

I rest my tired head on two pillows,
begging the day's creatures to let me sleep.
It is midnight, and must be dawn where you are.
The pulse travels faster than the light.
Which side are you sleeping on?

I feel my right arm
sheltering your face;
you smile a knowing smile,
one I would pocket if I went to war.

We are as happy as when we met.
I don't know whether we are young or old,
but my head nestles next to yours—
on one pillow.

The Two Angels

Among the things mother told me
as a child:

Every person has two angels
standing on his shoulders.
And they weigh every deed.
On the right, *Nakir*,
for the good deeds;
for the bad, *Nakeer*,
on the left.

That is why my gait is tilted now
and as the years pass—
my back will grow hunched.

Such nakedness!

In Balance

I was powerless against you then—
you noticed only my violations.
Now we stand in balance
in the brass pans of the scale,
and I sit next to you,

marvel at how the sun baked your face
black, simple, tenacious,
and how from the good earth,
the earth you made good,
your heart grew tender
as the hands rough.

Father, this apricot tree so lush,
climbing madly toward the sky,
yet bears no apricots.
She must be infatuated with herself.
Father, the grapevine in Uncle's garden
speaks no grapes.
She must be in mourning
over his death, he planted her.
Father, why don't you like the city?
I like to look undistracted
at the sky, to see the face of God.

But I Heard the Drops

My father had a reservoir
of tears.
They trickled down
unseen.
But I heard the drops
drip
from his voice
like drops from a loosened tap.
For thirty years
I heard them.

No Flowers for Flowers' Sake

I cannot understand the sublime,
patrician ways of the flowers.
Cannot tell when a rose is sick,
or why a pansy
doesn't answer my questions.

I count before I pluck the daisy's petals,
for I prefer the illusion of "she loves me"
over the despair of "not."

I had to wait many years
for my petite Chinese friend
to point out how the tulips in Washington
were so large, like American women.

And the hyacinth—I first met the hyacinth
in Eliot's wasteland, wasting.
Then I saw her in a real garden,
and she looked more like a bird
than a flower, a bird that had stopped,
suddenly, in mid-flight,
and its pent-up energy blazed
into a filigree of brilliance.

I could blame my being such a philistine on my parents
who grow olives and pears and figs and whatnot.
The blossoms of their orange trees are only a prelude
to the fruit. No flowers for flowers' sake.
The most abstract plant around their house is mint.

But I don't. I just bury my head
underground, like a potato,
to hide my form, which I better leave
without adjectives, and let my flesh feed
on the sumptuous dirt and darkness.

Me and Picasso

He couldn't swim,
according to *Picasso:*
Portrait of the Artist as a Young Man.
Neither can I.

He was shorter
and much bulkier than me.
And he loved boxing,
but loathed being punched.
In the only duel I've ever had
my drunk opponent knocked me out,
flat on the ground.

The painter's rigid, un-curved physique,
had the grace of a turtle
on the dance floor.
At a school function
my little son once begged me,
"Dad, can you do me a favor, please,
don't dance."

Jealousy drove him
to lock his lover in the studio
until one day a fire ate the place
and nearly killed her.
I would never go this far!

He felt at home
only in the austere hills of Andalusia,
inhaling the harsh odors of thyme.
On most mornings
I fortify my breakfast plate
with blue-green *za'atar*
from the rocky hills of Palestine.

Wouldn't he exchange
a few days in the grave
for some of mine?

Soliloquy

When I was a boy I didn't want to die
before a woman with a candid body
filled my arms,
her tongue danced with my tongue,
her teeth crashed with my own
and passion flowed between us in the slow night.

When the likeness of her came
I was in college, away from home,
and I leapt out of bed
each time I thought I could die
and be flown back in a box,
unable to wave for my father at the airport
and hand him my fresh, family diploma.

Alas, there are always reasons for living.

I have now causes that lose,
poems I've failed to write,
a wife and children—a counterweight.
It's almost midnight, and they are asleep.
I am downstairs, in the living room,
rocking in the rocking chair,
smoking a pipe. I stuff the bowl,
a pinch at a time,
sniff the aroma, and strike a match.
I bask, like the smoke, in my own dissolution.

Last night my dead cousin called
and said he and grandmother had found a house,
a pleasant white house on a hilltop,
then asked me to join them for dinner.
Tomorrow I'll race up and down
            the steep
                subway
                    stairs
                        to test
        .   my breath.

PART THREE

*He [Odysseus] saw many cities and learned
the thoughts of many men.*
—Italo Calvino

Roots

Home is where people can read your name correctly
on the tombstone.
—Attila József

At birth my parents called me
Sharif Said Hussein Elmusa
and on and on—a caravan of names
lagging behind
as if to rein me in from straying
on the crooked routes.

But one night, on a high balcony
under a full, urban moon,
a mountain woman
from the Rockies held me
in the clear pond of her eyes,
as if I was the first Adam.
And I followed love.

Uncle Sam,
casual and efficient,
inventor of the T-shirt,
that simplifier of the race,
found my name baroque,
bulging with self-importance,
yanked out grandfather
and downsized father
even before old age

to an initial, S.
Then the editors finished the job,
excised the atavistic S.
and left me to dream—
like someone who had lost his paradise—
I walked in stealth
in the city streets, with bare feet,
and only my underwear on.

See, my incurable yen
to keep going or coming
to Damascus and Rabat
Cairo and Amman
is not just turning the other cheek.
There, the security men at the border
keep their rugged names and moustaches,
scrutinize my left-to-right passport,
and poke fun at me for going back home
to Washington. They never fail
to ask about my father's name;
and I savor enunciating it:
Said Hussein.

More satisfying, still,
are the gatekeepers of Israel.
How they relish information.
They don't let go
until they had dug up,
among other things,
the names of my birth place,
the village their fathers

and grandfathers had taken
and re-configured, dwellings and name;
until they had dug up my known lineage
right down to the clan.

       Call me
            Sharif.

My Stella Beer T-shirt Tries to Come out
of the Closet

While loitering one day in the bazaar
I saw a white Stella Beer T-shirt,
liked it at first sight
and bought it without much bargaining.
It is made of the finest Egyptian cotton,
almost silk-thin and flannel to the touch.
On the left breast and back, a handsome logo
in Arabic and English calligraphy,
the words of the man who announced the death of God,
"That which does not kill us makes us stronger,"

Stella "local" is the beer that beer buffs,
natives and expats, hold in high esteem.
"It tastes home," Dina says,
the bottle is twice the size of the can,
and the wobbly pound goes a long way.
In all, a stellar brew of the land
that once made solemn offerings
of beer to the supreme gods.

But when the time comes
for wearing the shirt, my feet balk,
as if disabled by mother's,
imshi elhait elhait
"Walk alongside the wall, the wall,
and implore the Lord for safety."
I am afraid a keeper of the promise,

who has not read his Khayyam
who craves the everlasting wine
of Paradise, I am afraid he might be affronted
by the impious design, foam in rage
and stun my passing pleasure.

So I wear the shirt indoors,
after work, around the happy hour,
doubly savoring my Stellas.

But being a T-shirt and Egyptian
it has a social metabolism too strong to curb.
It is the first to fling itself
into the pagan suitcase shuttling back
to America, the origin of its kind,
even though it knows
the easy-going habitat that conceived it
is in the grip of uninflected fantasies
in the grip of the one-hundred-percent loyal.
They gaze at the olive skin,
at the broad lips of my mother tongue,
they gaze from their eagle's height,
with reptilian fear.

I hate them. I hate them all who made me write such
a high-pitched confessional about a closet affair.
I want my eccentricity to drift
without leaving a footprint on the paved streets.
If I were my daughter's age, I'd join a march
and hand the bullies confusing flowers.

I loathe my own capitulation even more.
I conjure bizarre schemes—
like going incognito,
as an American woman in Cairo
is said to have done, shielding
her upper body with a cardboard box,
to mark a sovereign space
against men's long arms and tongues.

Dispirited, unable to exceed my size,
I hear myself repeat,
"That which does not kill us makes us stronger."

Transit at Charles de Gaulle Airport

How could luminous Paris
birth such a loveless airport?

We, whose destination is the Third World,
are bussed to terminal 2E,
for 45 minutes—flight time to Milan.
The mutant vehicle, like a French theorist,
meanders incomprehensibly on a twisted road—
sharp turns, sudden stops,
no transitions between the curves; meanders
among bleak post-structures, aerodynamic
forms, as if meant as decoys
for the missiles of the former Soviet Union.

De Gaulle would have circumvented all,
like an American, with a shortcut.

I scan faces from the five continents,
a disparate collection of creatures,
looking lost as I always imagined the dead would be
on the first day of resurrection, no one knows anyone else,
yet somehow sense they are going somewhere.

I am a mortal cussing the fierce gatekeepers,
cussing the long march to the gates,
my rage is as vast as Gaul.

Ah, to be flown to my desert—duty-free.

How Odd These Amphibians

When the water pools dried,
the water dwellers would die—
according to A.S. Romer—
until, over slow, methodical time,
their fins branched out into legs,
not to fit them for living on land
but to take them back to water.

We go back to the water
where we were baptized
in jets and trains, go there
with laser eyes and lawyers' ears,
with tongues sporting new tentacles.

When we meet those who stayed
themselves, we put on airs
and mock their simple fins,
and they, they stare at us
with slanted eyes:
"How odd these amphibians,
what shall we do about them?"

Snapshots

Amman is softer / than the skin of goats
                              —A Bedouin poet

In the blink of an eye
flesh and cement
take over the ancient hills.

No river wets its throat.
The wisps of grass
turn yellow
under the first footfalls
of summer,

and the few birds
that come by
look puzzled, pained
like migrant workers.

Up and down the steep hills
cars, humped like camels,
issue their pleas.

In the minarets
God gets used
to loudspeakers.

Expatriates

The moon, neither full nor crescent, leans
35° toward the plane of melancholy. Jupiter
is missing, in its place a space for pondering.
Two anonymous stars leap from the constellation,
hand in hand. Blackberries fill the dipper.

A meteor falls mad,
in the blaze van Gogh, Attila József,
martyred for the nation of poetry.
Whereas Neruda pushes the walls of his trench
underground, still refusing to die.

I intend to live my ration of years and hours,
no more, no less. And when my boots grow heavy
I will think how that caterpillar
wove her cocoon on the sand of the beach,
how a nun might giggle riding a Ferris wheel.

Sun Lines

In his last days in Italy
Nietzsche wrote to a friend:
"When you're lonely
you become
friends with the sun."

Is the field of sunflowers a lonely crowd?

Why does the snake go into long sleep
when the sun orbits faraway?

Whom does a lonely man in a dark
Siberian winter take for a friend?

Was the architect who dreamed the obelisk
lying, lonely, under a palm tree?

Mohammad received his first word
from Gabriel in the cave.

The loneliness of Jesus led him to Golgotha.

I don't know much about the Buddha,
but his visage looks bathed in sunrays.

How far can we trust the thoughts
of lonely men?

The lovers opt for the moonlight.

How Things Migrate

The little calculator is lying
on the cushion on the couch,
a black box,
a sarcophagus of Pythagoras,
the lover of numbers,
of anorexic beauty.

The spineless pantyhose are
crumbled under the dining table
tired of standing erect,
buffering the cold wind.

How things migrate,
not wanting to be where they belong.
The militant bananas are mellowing
over the warm radiator. The caps
of the shampoo bottles and toothpaste
have vanished, en masse,
perhaps feeling guilty for being
the lids on free expression.

Where did the can opener go?
and the sharp knife?—the instruments
that do unto others.
And this stray cloud, hanging
in the half-open door,
is it coming in or going out?

I am a migrant, too,
and not the one
to put things in their place;
but this is not a surrealist canvas.
The guests with neat glasses
are coming.

Aren't We All Brothers?

So these are the hills of the Highlands,
mist and locks and monsters
sheep and heather and scarce sun
and people mumbling,
not the bare hills I had imagined
when, roaming the flat, barren land
east of the camp and, from a folded book
tucked in my back pocket, I memorized
"wherever I wander, wherever I roam,
the hills of the Highlands, for ever I love,"
these are the hills,
and we are rolling down
on narrow country roads
in a rental car
that my friend drove
because, being a man of habit,
and a bit timid,
I would not drive on the left side,
nor did I begrudge the British their quirks,
pounds and miles, although they
begrudged me my country,
and they trampled everyone's eccentricity,
and I had my friend, an indomitable American,
who drove cars when she was in the womb,
and Scotland for her was a small place,
and she took charge of the wheel,
and I felt safe next to her
and the whole thing was romantic

who cared about a car capsizing,
until, at a bend in the road,
she lurched into a ditch, exactly
as I had feared,
and here we were, feeling helpless,
when suddenly a young boy,
almost my age when I memorized
Bobby Burns's rhyme,
approached us, and looked
at the wheel stuck in the ditch
and said to wait a minute
and ran back and fetched his father,
driving a tractor,
and the man greeted us
and hooked the car to the tractor
which, like a benevolent monster,
lifted the car and our spirits,
and now the odd moment,
should we just thank him for his kindness
or pay him for his labor,
and we offered to "compensate" him,
but he demurred,
"Aren't we all brothers?"
sounding convinced and true
like a field of heather,
and we thanked them both,
as profusely as the falling rain
and said we'd love to visit again.

The Faisal-Jesus Bust

Is it still standing in that bed-size yard
or was it sent to the incinerator—
the olive-wood bust
I had bought from a tourist shop in Amman,
thinking that—with its Arab-like headdress
and thin goatee, puckered lips
and look of a man ill-at-ease—
it was a bust of king Faisal of Saudi Arabia,
a perfect image of the unhappy times
in the Middle East, carved
from the tree that once meant peace.

I hauled it from Boston to Washington
from Banks Street, Park Road
to Hobart Street. I kept it shiny,
free of dust, as if to remind it of who it was.

Until one day the Mexican couple next door
informed us, with some grave gestures,
someone had stolen the Madonna
from their front yard. We wondered why
anyone would do such a wicked thing,
and told them we were really sorry.
What else could we do.

Later my wife asked me
to give them the figure of Jesus,
"the one you brought from Jordan."

She, a Protestant, could not see why
we had kept it all these years.
"He's not Jesus," I said,
"he's king Faisal."
"Oh no! Just look at the crown of thorns."
"This is the headdress," I said,
and we laughed out loud.

So the next time we saw them
we offered our Catholic neighbors
the Faisal-Jesus bust.
They welcomed the gift
with tender hands, signs of the cross,
and wishes for peace in the Holy Land.
Soon after they built a little grotto
on the spot of the Madonna
and placed the bust inside it.

A Little Piece of Sky

Marveling today at the Safeway's abundance
of tuna fish cans,
I thought of my friend Hussein.
He was the genius of the school.
He breathed in history, grammar, math
as easily as the dust of the camp.
He had a pyramid's core. Books
would've sprouted from his head,
but he had to live, and to live he
apprenticed with a carpenter,
and later on flew the skill to an oil country
where he made good as a contractor.

His father had been killed the spring he was born
in a war that made us refugees
and tossed us on the moral map of the world.
His mother was a woman of meager means,
"Could look at a word for a year
and not recognize what it was."
And so it was:
Poverty wagged him everyday.

One afternoon
I met him walking home from the store
holding, with his thumb and forefinger,
the upright lid of a half-opened
tuna fish can, humming a tune
about holding a little piece of sky.

Haven't You Found My Brother in America?

As if thirty years haven't gone by
since the young boy succumbed
to the whirlpool in the Jordan River
As if the soccer ball he passed to me
hasn't exhaled its poor air
inside the goal of oblivion
As if the pine trees we climbed
have stayed evergreen
As if the dark basalt rocks
guarding the river haven't ceased
to echo his mother's cry
As if I haven't fled five thousand miles away
His younger sister showed up last night
and leaned on the edge of my sleep
and with a severe look in her eyes
and a demanding voice, she said to me:
"Haven't you found my brother in America?"

Yearning

To build is to collaborate with time.
—Marguerite Yourcenar, *Memoirs of Hadrian*

I could tell you the number
or describe the pattern of the wallpaper
and the desk between the two beds—
but this is a hotel room.
It is not meant to be observed.
Its beige air cannot retain
kisses, coughs or pain.
Tomorrow it'll be bulldozed
and no one will inherit it.
It could be in Chicago or Taipei.
The universal imagination has set in—
the imagination of economic man
whose numbers are his romance,
who sees sin in color
and virtue in the line,
who lets in no demons
other than his own.

I am a yearner
conceived out of yearning.
I want to feel
the walls warm from being touched
by long-vanished hands.
I want to feel the city lights
shine as if from the firmament.

I want to kneel and sing
some refined praise.
But even the moon tonight leans
like a derelict
against the brick-walled sky.
My beige spirit begs to be wounded.

Homeward Bound

Dozing off on the train late in the evening,
I miss my stop. I am tired
and can hardly walk up the stairs
to the opposite side.
I think of the old man telling me
how he used to walk for three or four hours
in the field, then hold the calves of his legs
and ask each of them if it could do more.
My legs feel his legs as they climb.

I loiter around the gray platform.
A man inspects a cigarette butt
with an almost admiring attitude
then crushes it gently under his shoe.
A man and a woman talk of going
on a long journey south, perhaps inspired
by the full desert moon.
In this station faraway from downtown
there are no astonished statues
of Ancient Egyptians
reminding you how it is all out of joint.

Trying to lean against a wall
I see a file of ants running fiercely
up and down along a crack in the cement.
The ones crawling down haul tiny pieces
of straw; the ones ascending aim for the store.
Their dark bodies, shiny under a strong light,

touch on the run. None lingers or strays.
What drives them, patience or hope?
Don't their legs balk?

The body pokes the meddling mind
to mind its own business. It pricks up
its ears to listen for the sweet rumble
of the train. It craves the wide bed,
and the absent woman
to crawl beside.